# ROCKS AND MINERALS OF THE WORLD

**SPEEDY**
PUBLISHING

Speedy Publishing LLC
40 E. Main St. #1156
Newark, DE 19711
www.speedypublishing.com

All rocks are made of
two or more minerals,
but minerals are not
made of rocks.

Granite is an igneous rock. Granite is one of the hardest substances in the world. Granite is considered the most abundant basement rock on the Earth.

Granite has been extensively used as a dimension stone and as flooring tiles in public and commercial buildings and monuments.

Limestone is a sedimentary rock. Limestone can most abundantly be found in the shallow ends of marine water.

Limestone is often used in construction such as being added to paint as a thickening agent.

Marble is a metamorphic rock. Marble usually lays among the oldest part of the Earth's crust.

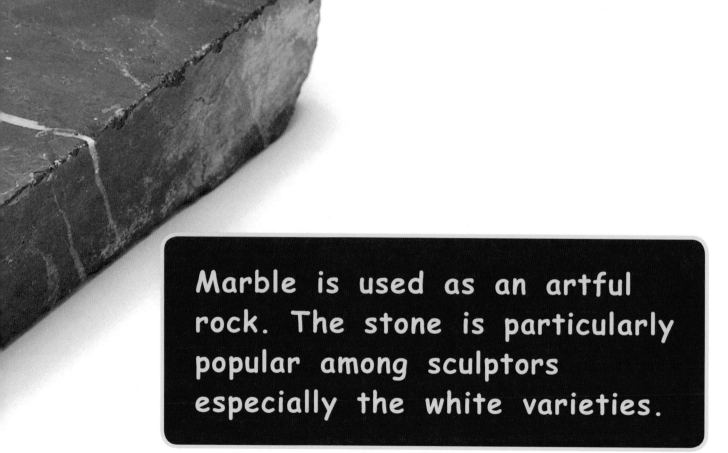

Marble is used as an artful rock. The stone is particularly popular among sculptors especially the white varieties.

5730 a

11.260

3.51 d

enstoff 3550

.0855

29

4.7

2.2

31(β⁻)

ö

.70

60.4

14 Si

Silicium

64

Aluminum is a silvery-white, soft, nonmagnetic, ductile metal. It is the most abundant metal found naturally on Earth.

Aluminum is globally the most used metal that does not contain iron. One of the most popular uses of aluminum is packaging.

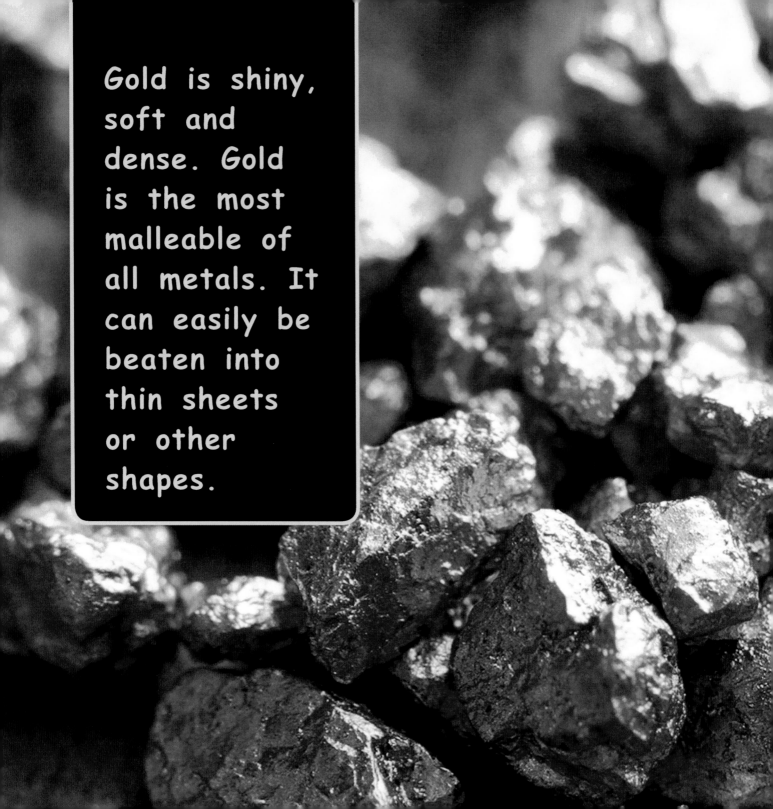

Gold is shiny, soft and dense. Gold is the most malleable of all metals. It can easily be beaten into thin sheets or other shapes.

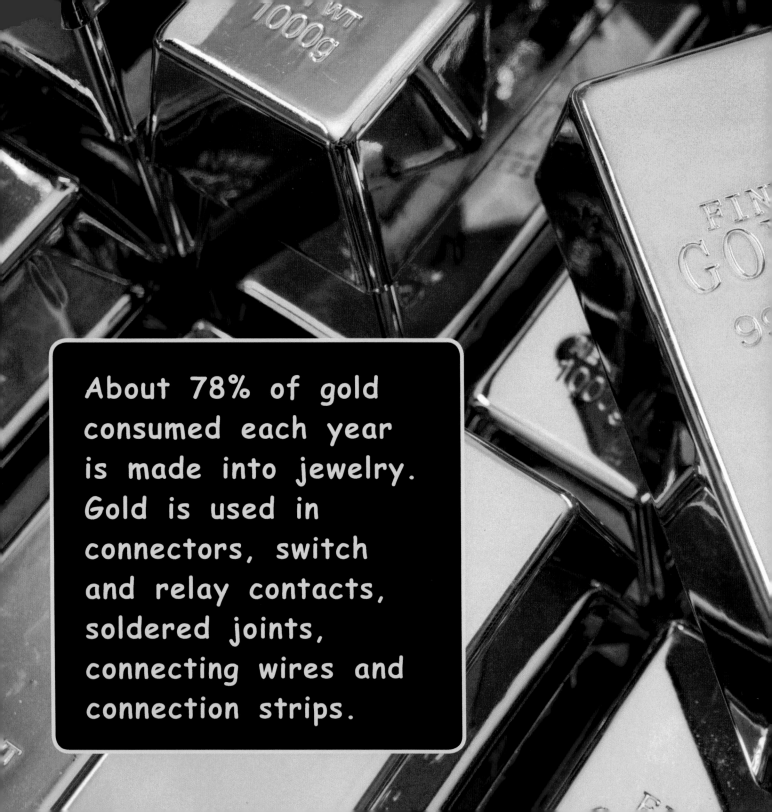

About 78% of gold consumed each year is made into jewelry. Gold is used in connectors, switch and relay contacts, soldered joints, connecting wires and connection strips.

Silver has the highest electrical conductivity of all the elements. Silver was one of the first metals discovered by ancient peoples.

Silver is precious metal that has been used for many years to make fine pieces of jewelry, coins and utensils.

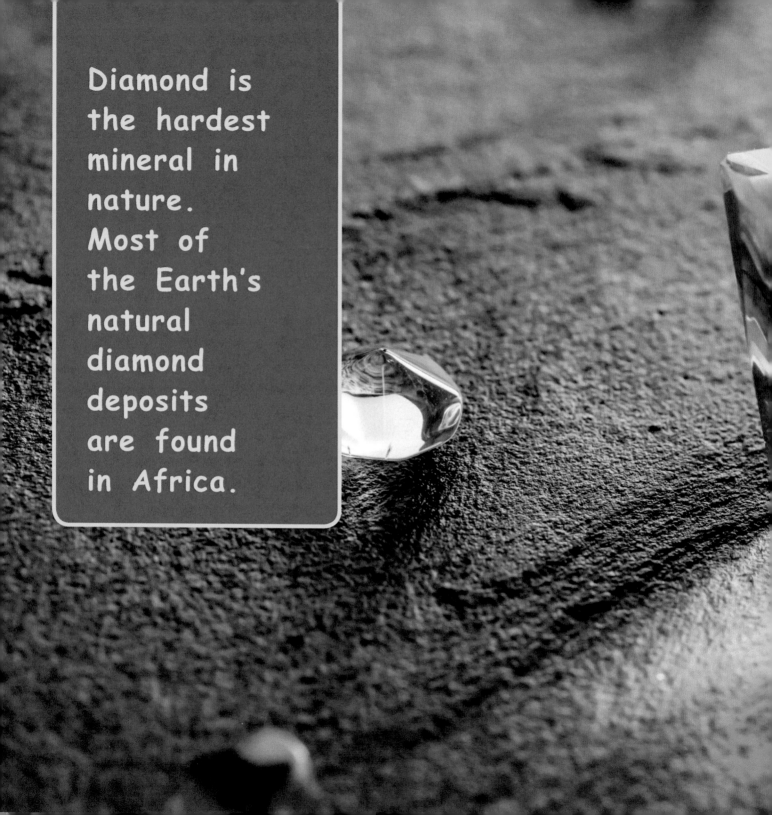

Diamond is the hardest mineral in nature. Most of the Earth's natural diamond deposits are found in Africa.

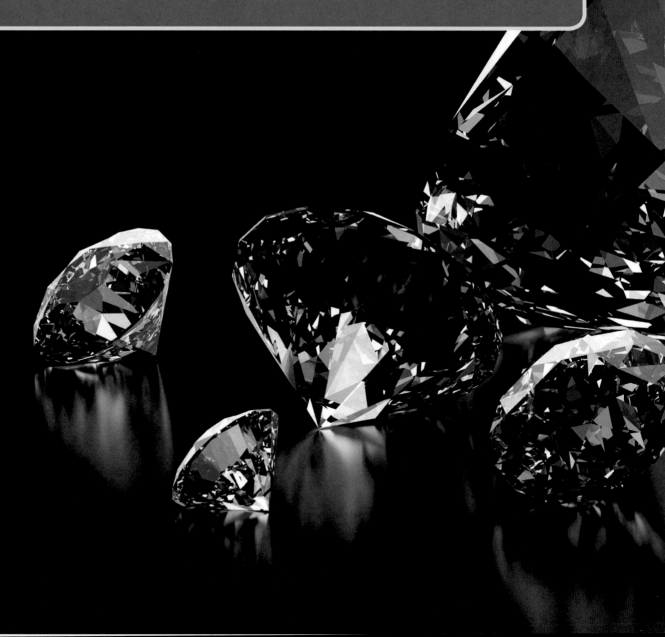

Diamonds are used to make jewelry. It is also used to cut, grind and bore into other hard materials.

Made in the USA
Coppell, TX
26 May 2020